WILLIAM SHAKESPEARE'S

Macbeth

RETOLD BY   ILLUSTRATED BY

BRUCE COVILLE   **GARY KELLEY**

MACDONALD YOUNG BOOKS

34,596

*For all the courageous actors who have braved
"the curse" to keep this play alive – B.C.*

For my Lady Linda – G.K.

First published in 1997 by Dial Books
A Division of Penguin Books USA Inc
375 Hudson Street
New York
New York 10014

First published in Great Britain in 1998
by Macdonald Young Books
an imprint of Wayland Publishers Ltd
61 Western Road
Hove
East Sussex
BN3 1JD

A catalogue record for this book
is available from the British Library.

The artwork was prepared with pastels on paper.

ISBN 0 7500 2544 1

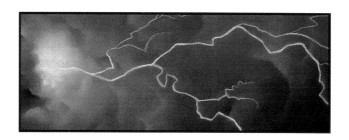

Author's Note

When you speak of *Macbeth* in theatrical circles, it is preferred that you call it "The Scottish Play". This is because the play is considered to be cursed, and actors' lore has it that you must never mention the title inside a theatre. If you *do* slip and say "Macbeth" aloud, there are actions you must take to ward off the evil thus invited in! Curse or no curse, it didn't prevent Abraham Lincoln from declaring it his favourite of Shakespeare's plays.

While *Macbeth* may make actors nervous, it remains one of the most popular, and most frequently performed, of all Shakespeare's works. A horrific tale of witches, murder, ghosts, and revenge, it deals poetically with many of the elements popular with young readers – which makes it a perfect avenue for introducing them to the Bard. Within the story the reader will find some of the most often quoted lines in the English language – which is one reason for this adaptation.

Because Macbeth is one of the shortest of Shakespeare's plays, it has been possible to include here virtually all the elements of the plot. The sections I have most sharply abbreviated are the porter scene – which can be screamingly funny on stage when played by the right clown, but is more about philosophy than plot; Malcolm's testing of Macduff, which is frequently cut in performance as well; and the actual slaughter of Macduff's family.

As in my other adaptation of Shakespeare – *A Midsummer Night's Dream* – the real goal is to offer young readers a sense of the pleasure that awaits them in these plays. Possibly more than any other writer, the Bard bears the curse of greatness – a reputation that leads many people to an ill-founded fear that the writing is "too hard". Early exposure to Shakespeare's stories is one way to inoculate against that idea, and to build a natural interest in the plays themselves – an interest that can lead to a lifetime of reading and viewing enjoyment.

Thunder shook the skies over Scotland. War raged across the heath as the Scottish thanes fought to turn back invaders from Ireland and Norway. Striding fearlessly through the battle, his flashing sword red with blood, was the greatest warrior of the day – Macbeth, Thane of Glamis. No foe could stand against him.

When the battle was finally won, Macbeth and his friend Banquo headed for the king's castle. An eerie fog swirled thick about them, dampening their great victory. "So foul and fair a day I have not seen," said Macbeth.

"Fouler still as the day goes on," said Banquo, "for what are these dark shapes huddled before us?"

Warily the men drew up their horses. In their path stood three witches, withered and wild-looking.

"All hail Macbeth, Thane of Glamis," said the first.

"All hail Macbeth, Thane of Cawdor," croaked the second.

"All hail Macbeth, who shall one day be king," hissed the third.

Macbeth was startled into silence, but Banquo chided him. "Why fear what sounds so fair?" Then he turned to the weird three and said, "If you can look into the seeds of time, and say which grain will grow and which will not, then speak to me of what my life shall be."

"Lesser than Macbeth, and greater," said the first witch.

"Not so happy, yet much happier," murmured the second.

"Thou shalt be the father of kings, though thou be none," said the third.

"So all hail Macbeth and Banquo!" they screeched together, and then faded into the murky air.

"Your children shall be kings," said Macbeth at last, his voice thick with awe.

"*You* shall be king!" replied Banquo.

"And Thane of Cawdor too, went it not so?"

Filled with wonder, the two men journeyed on. In time they heard hoofbeats approaching, and out of the fog appeared two messengers sent by King Duncan. The first of them, spotting Macbeth, called, "Hail, Thane of Cawdor!"

Macbeth shivered on hearing this, the very title the second witch had called him! "Why do you dress me in borrowed robes?" he asked. "The Thane of Cawdor lives."

"Not for long," said the messenger. "He has betrayed the king and is condemned to die. His land and title come from Duncan's hand to thee, in gratitude for your great deeds in today's battle, which many reports have brought to the king's ear."

So the weird three spoke the truth about Cawdor, thought Macbeth. What other truths might they have spoken? They called me king, did they not? On this day of battle the chance seemed especially strong. For it was a time when the crown often passed not to the king's son but to the kingdom's greatest warrior.

Banquo, seeing a strange look in his friend's eyes, cautioned, "Be not too eager. Remember, the powers of darkness may use a bit of truth to lure a man to doom."

When the men made camp that night, Macbeth wrote to his wife, telling her all that had happened. Then he lay awake for a long time, thinking of what the witches had foretold… and more. The darkness of the night mirrored his thoughts. Thoughts of the throne and the quickest route to it. Murderous thoughts. He struggled with them until a fitful sleep came to him at last.

The next day Macbeth and Banquo reached Dunsinane Castle, where they found Duncan delighted to see them. "Oh, worthiest cousin!" cried the king. "More is due you than I can pay."

"To serve you is payment in itself," said Macbeth humbly.

"I have begun to plant thee," said the king, "and will labour to make thee full of growing. Tonight I shall away to your castle, so that we may celebrate."

"For this great honour, my thanks," said Macbeth. "I will ride ahead, to give my wife the joyful news that you are coming."

At Macbeth's castle, Inverness, Lady Macbeth pored over her husband's letter. The witches' prediction that he would be king set her mind churning. She paced her chambers for a long time, thinking of all that might be. "Yet I do fear your nature, my husband," she muttered. "It is too full of the milk of human kindness for you to catch the nearest way. I shall have to urge thee on, to do what must be done."

Lady Macbeth was deeply absorbed in her reverie, when she heard a familiar footstep. She turned to find her husband at the door.

"My dearest love," he said, "Duncan comes here tonight."

"Tonight," she said, her heart stirring. "And when does he leave?"

"Tomorrow."

The lady shook her head and whispered, "Never shall that morrow come, my lord."

Macbeth eyed her warily.

"Your face, my thane, is like a book where I may read strange matters. Let no one else see. Look like the innocent flower, but be the serpent under it. Leave all the rest to me."

The castle was abustle with excitement over Duncan's visit. Music and laughter filled the air. Fine food covered the tables. But Macbeth stole away, troubled by thoughts of the terrible crime he and his wife were slipping toward.

"The king is here in double trust," he muttered. "He is both my guest, and my kinsman. I should bar the door against his murderer, not bear the knife myself."

While he tried to talk himself out of the bloody deed, his wife appeared at his side. "Why have you left the feast?" she hissed.

"We will proceed no further in this business," said Macbeth.

"Are you afraid to claim your greatness?" his wife mocked. "Screw your courage to the sticking place! When Duncan is asleep, I will carry wine to his guards, as any hostess might. The wine will be drugged. Once the men are senseless, what cannot you and I perform on the unguarded Duncan? And all the guilt will fall upon his weak and spongy officers."

Macbeth was appalled by his wife's ferocity. Yet he would not appear a coward before her, and the lure of the throne was too powerful. Finally he said, "If we use the guards' own daggers for the deed, their guilt will be sealed."

His wife smiled. "Who would dare say else while we are weeping and mourning the crime?"

Macbeth took her hand. "It is settled then. Let us return to the feast. Smile and be merry. False face must hide what the false heart doth know."

The night drew on, moonless and without stars. The castle was asleep when Macbeth entered the courtyard, so intent on his bloody work that his mind began to conjure up images. "Is this a dagger I see before me?" he said in wonder. He clutched at it, but could not grasp it. Yet it drew him on, this dagger of the mind… on to Duncan's chambers.

Lady Macbeth had been there already: The guards were asleep with their daggers beside them. Now she waited nervously for her husband to finish the deed.

Suddenly she heard a cry from the king's chamber. Outside the castle an owl shrieked.

Then Macbeth was at her side, eyes wide, gasping for breath. " 'Tis done," he whispered. "But methought I heard a voice cry, 'Sleep no more. Macbeth doth murder sleep!'"

In his bloodstained hands he clutched a pair of daggers. Lady Macbeth was horrified. "Why did you bring these with you? Take them back. Smear the sleepy grooms with this blood. Then get some water and wash this filthy witness from your hands."

"I'll go no more. I am afraid to think what I have done. Look on it again I dare not."

"Infirm of purpose! Give me the daggers." Lady Macbeth snatched the knives and hurried off to do her grisly work.

In a moment there came a knocking at the castle gate. Macbeth heard it, but stood frozen, staring at his hands. "To wash them clean would turn the green seas red," he moaned.

The knocking continued, louder, and louder still.

When Lady Macbeth returned, her hands were as stained as her husband's. "Retire we to our chamber," she said, leading him away. "A little water will clear us of this deed."

More knocking, angry and insistent, echoed through the castle. Finally a drunken porter stumbled to the door, grumbling about the disturbance. In stormed two thanes, Macduff and Lennox by name. Newly washed, and garbed in nightclothes, Macbeth came to greet them.

"Is the king stirring yet?" Macduff asked. "He did bid me come early to his side."

"I'll bring you to him," said Macbeth. He led the men to the king's door, but left it to Macduff to go in and wake the old man.

While they waited, Lennox spoke of the unruliness of the previous night. "Chimneys were blown down," he said, "and strange screams of death seemed to fill the air."

" 'Twas a rough night," agreed Macbeth.

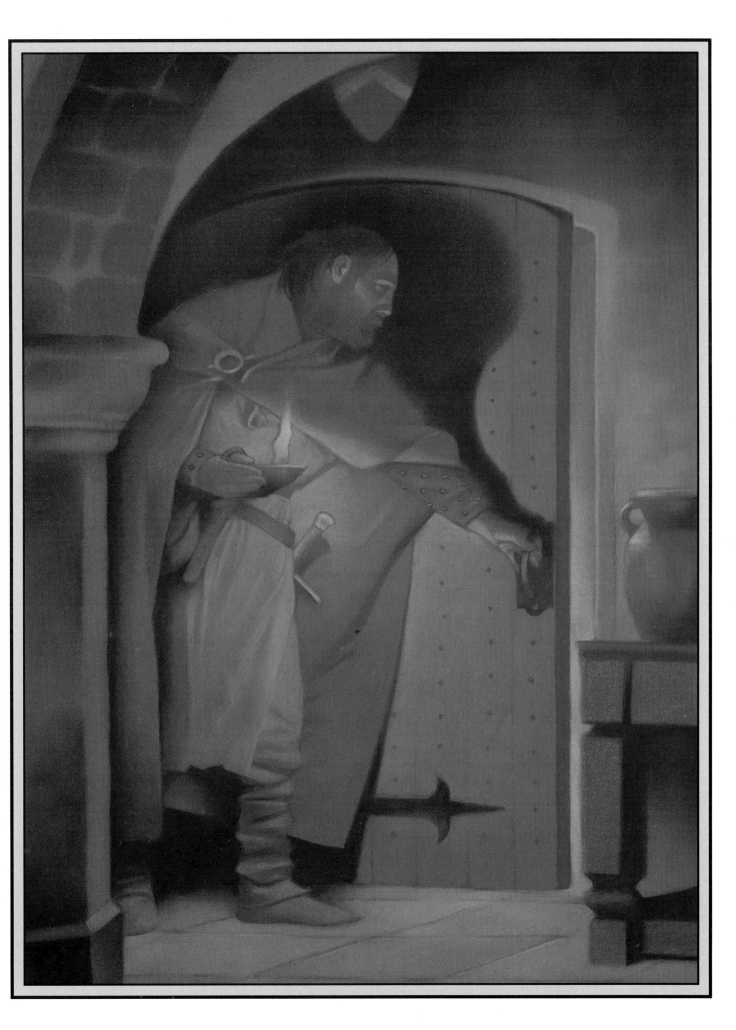

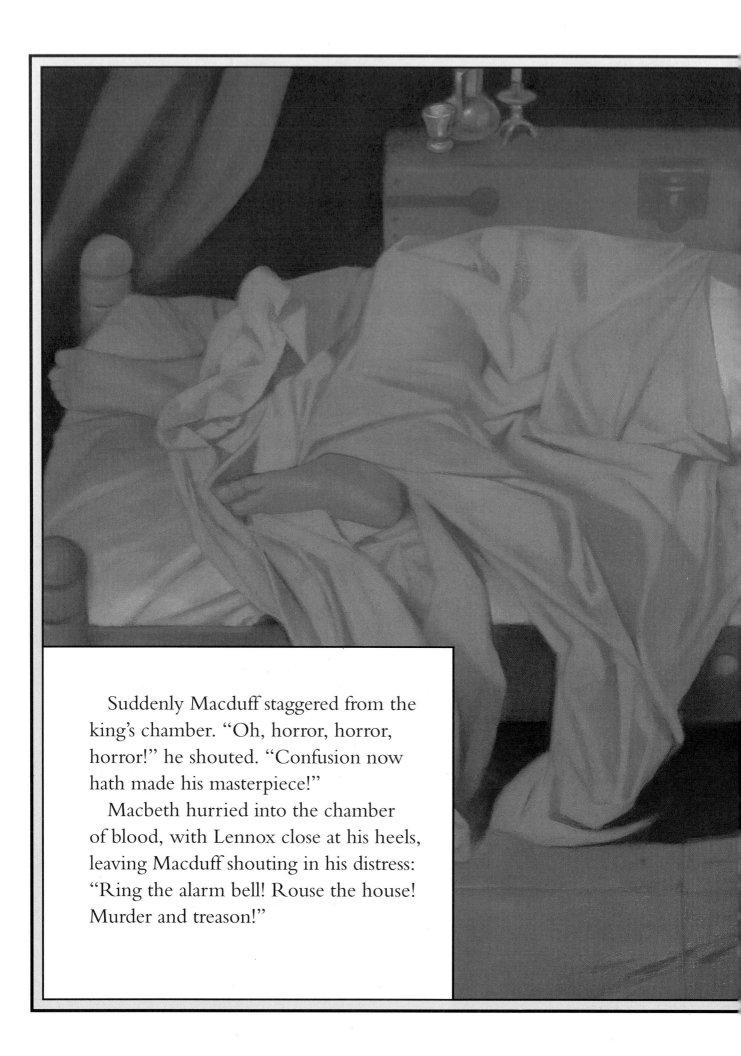

Suddenly Macduff staggered from the
king's chamber. "Oh, horror, horror,
horror!" he shouted. "Confusion now
hath made his masterpiece!"

Macbeth hurried into the chamber
of blood, with Lennox close at his heels,
leaving Macduff shouting in his distress:
"Ring the alarm bell! Rouse the house!
Murder and treason!"

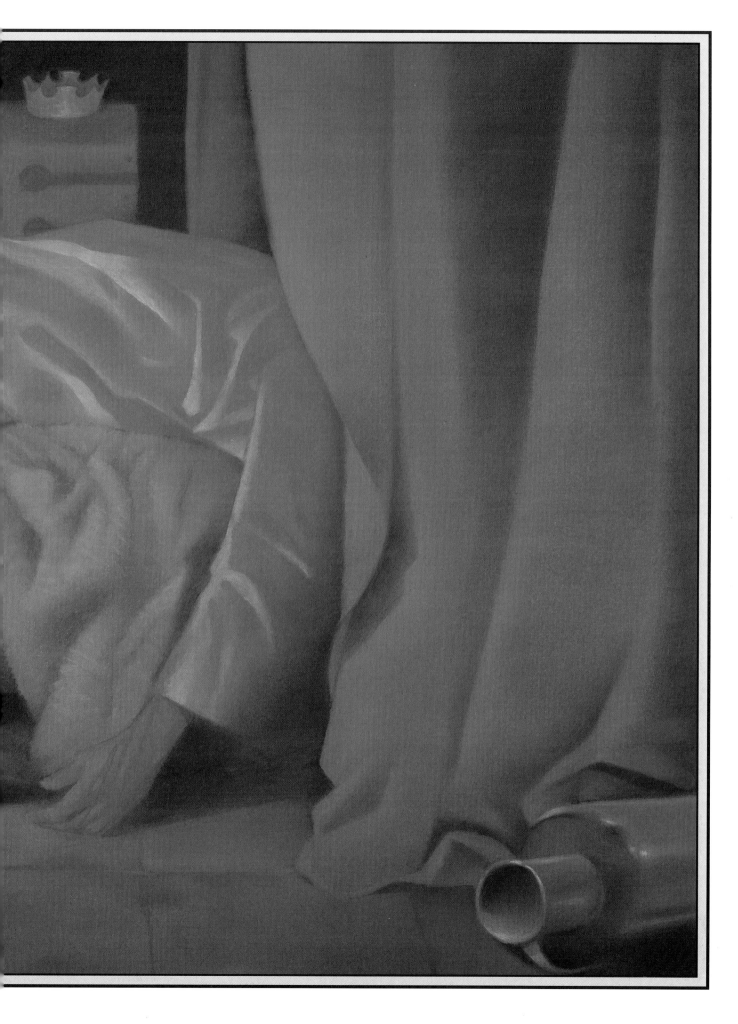

One by one, all who had accompanied the king hastened to the courtyard. Among them were the king's sons, Malcolm and Donalbain.

"What is amiss?" asked Donalbain.

"Your royal father is murdered!" wept Macduff.

"By whom?" cried Malcolm.

"It would seem the very men who were pledged to guard him," said Lennox as he and Macbeth returned to the courtyard. "Their hands and faces were smeared with his blood, as were their daggers."

"Yet I do repent me of my fury that I did kill them," said Macbeth.

"Wherefore did you so?" demanded Macduff.

"Who can be wise, amazed, temperate and furious, loyal and neutral in a moment?" replied Macbeth. "Here lay Duncan, laced with his golden blood. There lay his murderers. Who could refrain, that had a heart to love?"

Macduff eyed him with suspicion, but asked no further questions. There was too much to be done. The men agreed to dress quickly, then meet again in the courtyard.

But the king's sons hung behind. Like Macduff, they sensed that it was not the guards who had committed the crime. "Our father's murderer may want our blood as well," said Malcolm.

"True enough," said Donalbain. "In this place there are daggers in men's smiles. Better for us to leave. I'll to Ireland."

"And I to England."

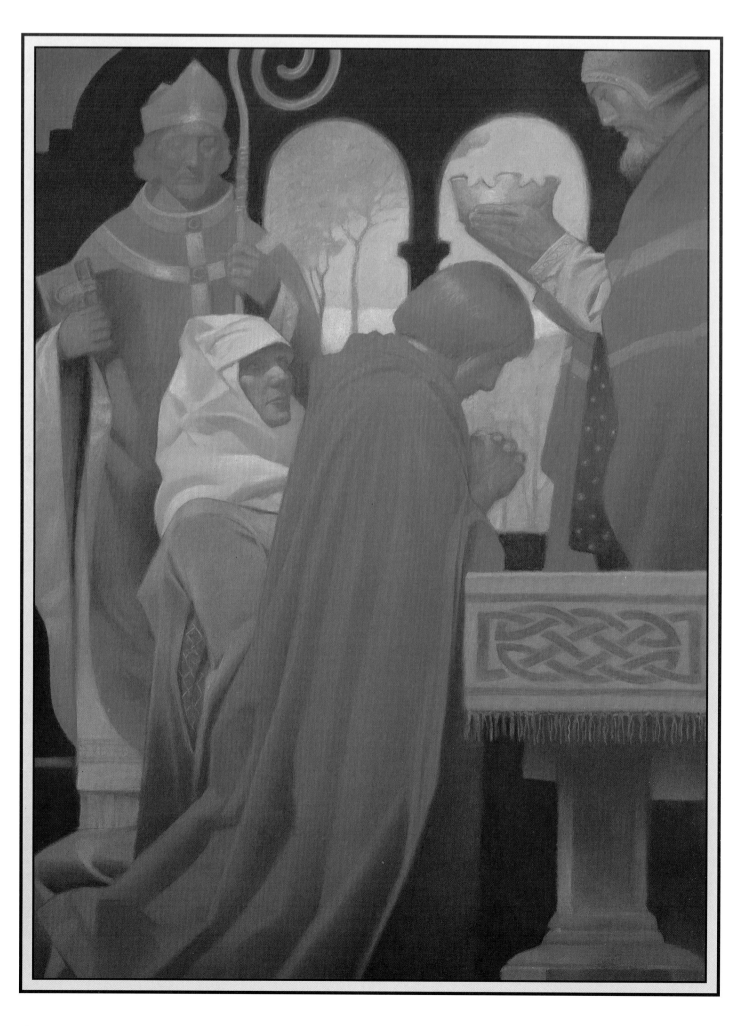

So the brothers fled to safety. But their very flight brought suspicion on them. The thanes decided that Malcolm and Donalbain must have urged the guards to do the murder, so they could early claim their father's throne. Now, with Duncan dead and his sons in exile, the thanes chose their greatest warrior to be king. They chose Macbeth.

But Macduff remained doubtful of the new king, and did not go to the coronation. Instead he returned to his wife and children at his home in Fife.

His absence did not go unnoticed by the king.

Macbeth and his lady, now rulers of Scotland, took up residence at Dunsinane. Yet the crown did not rest easy on the murderer's head, and his sleep was racked with guilty nightmares.

Adding to Macbeth's unrest was the knowledge that one man had true reason to suspect him of Duncan's murder: his old friend, Banquo, who had witnessed the weird sisters' prophecy that he would be king. And Macbeth could not forget their words foretelling that Banquo, not he, would be the father of kings.

"For Banquo's children have I sold my soul," he moaned. "For them have I murdered the gracious Duncan!"

The idea tormented Macbeth so fiercely that he finally decided both Banquo and his son Fleance must be killed, so Scotland's crown could never pass to their line.

With treachery in mind, Macbeth invited his friend to a banquet. On the afternoon of the great event, Banquo and his son took to their horses to explore the countryside surrounding Dunsinane. It was a pleasant day, with several hours before the banquet was to begin. But Macbeth had his friend followed by three men of murderous intent – men who had orders to kill both Banquo and Fleance.

That night the thanes gathered in Macbeth's great hall. He greeted them jovially, though he pretended to be worried about Banquo's absence. As the feast began, one of the murderers returned. He called the king aside and whispered, "Banquo is dead, but Fleance has escaped."

Another murder, thought Macbeth, and still he had not put an end to the witches' prophecy that Banquo would be the father of kings. But he masked his distress and returned to the feast, begging the thanes to join him in a toast. "To Banquo!" he cried. "How unkind of him not to be with us."

Even as Macbeth raised his glass, Banquo made good on his promise to attend. Bloody with the gashes the murderers had put upon him, his ghost drifted into the great hall.

The sight filled the king with cold horror. But the gathered thanes could not understand why he stared and stammered, for they saw no ghost, only the terrified Macbeth.

After a time the spirit vanished. Yet no sooner did Macbeth recover his wits than it reappeared. "Quit my sight!" pleaded the king. "Let the earth hide thee! Thy bones are marrowless, thy blood is cold. Hence, horrible shadow! Hence!"

Lady Macbeth tried desperately to calm him, all the while making excuses for his odd behaviour. But though the ghost finally left again, Macbeth was so shaken that his lady had to hurry the guests from the banquet hall.

In the months that followed, a darkness seemed to settle over Scotland. The gentle old king and the loyal Banquo had been murdered. The king's sons had fled, and of Banquo's son Fleance there was no trace. Too many deaths and disappearances were making the thanes suspicious of their new king, who was proving to be a moody and bitter ruler.

Rebellion was brewing, and Macbeth knew it. His spies whispered to him that Malcolm was stirring up an English army to free Scotland from Macbeth's bloody rule. Finally Macbeth decided to consult once more with the witches.

Out on the dark and blasted heath, the three witches wove their spells. Round about and round about their bubbling cauldron they danced, chanting…

"Double, double, toil and trouble,
Fire burn and cauldron bubble.
Eye of newt and toe of frog,
Wool of bat and tongue of dog,
For a charm of powerful trouble,
Like a hell-broth boil and bubble."

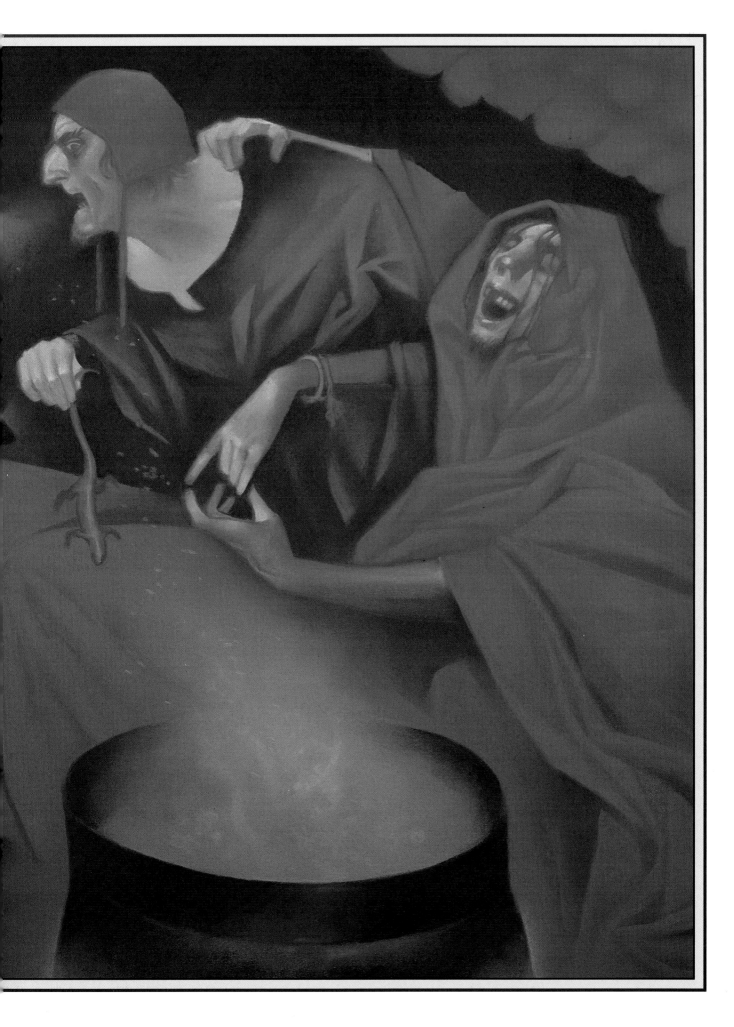

When the brew was complete, they danced again, bony fingers entwined, until one said, "By the pricking of my thumbs, something wicked this way comes."

Macbeth entered their cave. "How now, you secret midnight hags. What is it that you do?"

"A deed without a name," they replied in one voice.

"I come with questions," Macbeth said. "Now I conjure you to answer them, even if so doing will blast the world to pieces."

"Speak. Demand. We'll answer. Or would you rather hear it from our masters?"

"Call them," demanded Macbeth.

The weird sisters worked their magic. Sudden thunder split the sky, and out of the darkness an armoured head appeared.

"Macbeth, Macbeth, Macbeth," it said in ghastly tones. "Beware Macduff. Beware the Thane of Fife."

Macbeth nodded. "For this warning, thanks. But one word more—"

"He will not be commanded," said the first witch as the head vanished. "But here's another, even more potent."

Now appeared a bloody child. "Macbeth, Macbeth, Macbeth!" it chanted. "Be bloody, bold, and resolute; laugh to scorn the power of man, for none of woman born shall harm Macbeth."

"Then live, Macduff!" crowed the king. "What need I fear of thee? But wait… what is this that rises now?"

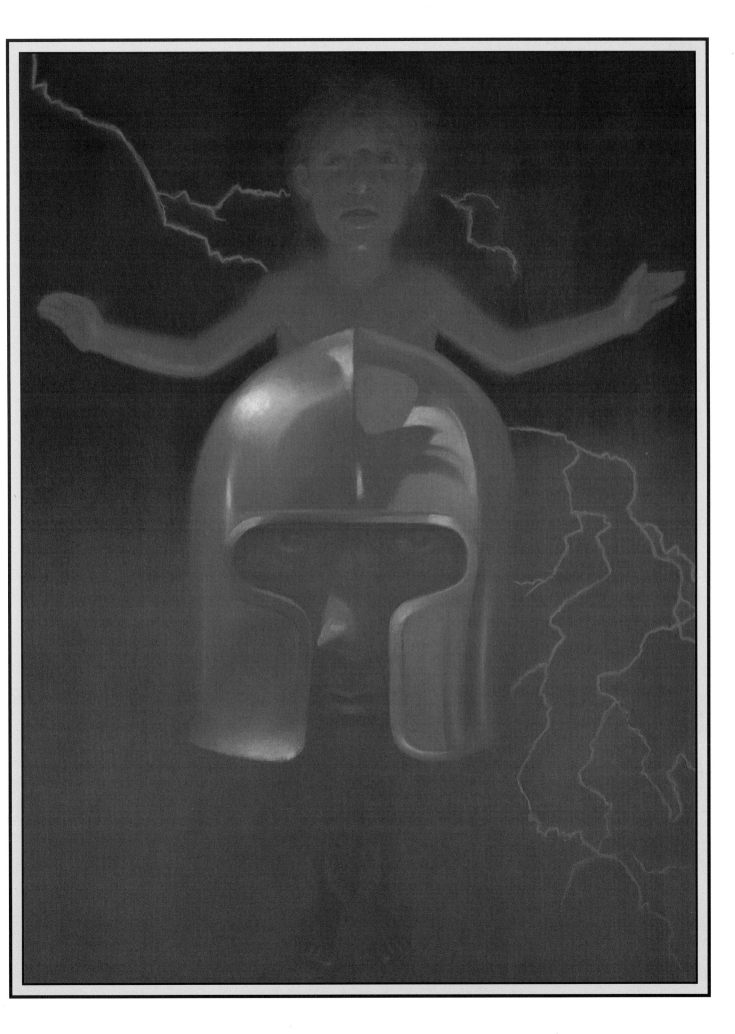

It was another child, wearing a crown and carrying a small tree. "Macbeth shall never vanquished be, until Great Birnam Wood to high Dunsinane Hill shall come against him."

"That will never be!" cried Macbeth happily. "For who can bid the trees pull their roots from the ground and walk?"

Still he insisted on asking one more question, the one that burned him in the night: "Shall Banquo's children ever reign in this kingdom?"

"Seek to know no more," warned the witches.

"Deny me this, and an eternal curse fall on you," said Macbeth. "Answer me!"

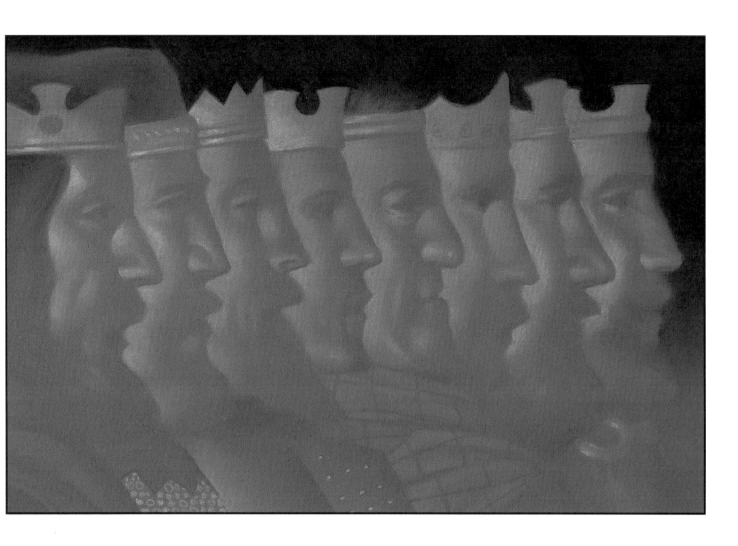

“Show, show, show,” murmured the witches. “Show his eyes and grieve his heart.” Then out of the shadows came a ghostly procession of eight kings, the last holding a mirror that showed many more. And walking with them was their forebear, Banquo.

The witches soon vanished, leaving Macbeth alone with his rage and sorrow. While he brooded thus, a messenger rode up.

“My lord,” said the messenger, “Macduff has fled to England.”

Macbeth was furious. “I should have acted the moment I suspected him a traitor. From this day my thoughts and deeds shall be as one.” Then he gave the bloody order: “Go to Fife. Enter Macduff’s castle. Put the traitor’s wife and children to the sword.”

In England good Macduff, unaware of the horrid calamity about to befall his family, was urging Malcolm to speed his return to Scotland. "You must reclaim your father's throne," he pleaded.

For a long time Malcolm resisted. When at last he did agree, he said, "I had to be sure of you, for Macbeth has sent many spies to lure me back – men who would have taken me home to die. I had to know you came for the sake of Scotland, rather than to betray me."

Macduff's heart lifted. This was the man who should be king!

But the Thane of Fife's joy was short-lived. By nightfall a messenger brought the dreadful news that Macduff's wife and babes had been slaughtered. "Did heaven look on, and would not take their part?" cried Macduff, near swallowed by grief. "Oh, now bring me front to front with this fiend of Scotland!"

"The time is coming," assured Malcolm. "Receive what cheer you may. Let us make medicines of our great revenge to cure this deadly grief."

But for some grief there is no cure. Lady Macbeth, consumed with guilt, had begun walking in her sleep. Rising from her bed, she would take up a candle and wander the castle, muttering strange words.

Finally one of her attendants summoned a doctor. They waited breathlessly in the darkened courtyard, and shortly after midnight the queen appeared. Setting down her candle, she began to rub her hands, slowly at first, then frantically. And as she rubbed, she moaned. "Out, damned spot – out I say! Who would have thought the old man to have had so much blood in him? What, will these hands never be clean? Here's the smell of blood still. Oh, all the perfumes of Arabia will not sweeten this little hand."

The doctor turned to the attendant. "Unnatural deeds breed unnatural troubles," he whispered. "I fear your lady's hands will not be made clean by any medicine I can offer."

Outside Dunsinane great forces were gathering. The English king had sent an army with Malcolm and Macduff to help overturn the tyrant. Macbeth knew from his spies that they were coming, yet he did not worry. Had not the spirits told him he would never be vanquished till Birnam Wood should come to Dunsinane?

Still he suffered, because for all the blood on his hands, the throne had offered him little happiness. Nor had it brought joy to his wife, who was sick unto dying with guilt.

"Canst thou not minister to a mind diseased?" he begged the doctor. "Pluck from memory a rooted sorrow, with some sweet antidote cleanse her of that which weighs upon her heart?" When the doctor told him nay, Macbeth called for his armour. He strapped it on with all the fervour he might use to battle his lady's sorrow.

Out in Birnam Wood, Malcolm ordered each man in his army to cut a branch from the trees. "Hold it before you. Thus we will approach Dunsinane without Macbeth knowing our true numbers!"

Macbeth was on the battlements, scanning the countryside for sight of the approaching army, when he heard a mournful cry from the women. Soon came a messenger with the news: "The queen, my lord, is dead."

Despair wrapped itself about the king. But his troubles came in full flood when a second messenger rushed in, choking on his words. "As I stood my watch upon the hill, I looked toward Birnam and . . . it seemed the wood began to move."

"Liar and slave!" roared Macbeth. "If thou speak'st false, upon the next tree shalt thou hang alive. If thy speech be true, I care not if thou do the same to me. Oh, I 'gin to grow aweary of the sun."

But his warrior heart insisted he fight on, and so he prepared to face his enemies.

The first of Malcolm's soldiers to find Macbeth was young and strong. Even so, he was easily vanquished. "Thou wast born of woman," scorned Macbeth, remembering the witches' prophecy. But as he pulled his sword from the lifeless soldier, he heard a cry from behind him: "Turn, hell-hound! Turn!"

Macbeth spun about. There stood Macduff, eyes blazing, chest heaving, sword raised for battle.

"Get thee back!" cried Macbeth. "My soul is too much charged with blood of thine already."

"I have no words," snarled Macduff. "My voice is in my sword, thou bloody villain."

Then swords rang out as the two great warriors fought with all their strength. "You waste your energy," panted Macbeth. "I bear a charmed life, which must not yield to one of woman born."

"Then despair," cried Macduff, "for I was not born as normal men, but cut too early from my mother's womb!"

Macbeth's heart sank. For now he realized that the spirits had played him false with their truths. Still he would not yield. Raising his bloody blade again he roared, "I will try the last. Lay on Macduff, and damned be him that first cries, 'Hold, enough!'"

Swords crashing and clanging they fought again, until at last Macduff ran his blade through the tyrant's heart. Then he severed Macbeth's head.

When he presented the prize to Malcolm before the gathering thanes, a mighty cheer rang out: "Hail, Malcolm! Hail, King of Scotland!"

Thus ended the dark and bloody reign of Macbeth, who killed a king to become a king, and in so doing murdered his own soul. Thus did a bright new day dawn in Scotland.